First World War
and Army of Occupation
War Diary
France, Belgium and Germany

52 DIVISION
Headquarters, Branches and Services
Royal Army Ordnance Corps
Deputy Assistant Director Ordnance Services
1 April 1918 - 30 April 1919

WO95/2891/3

The Naval & Military Press Ltd
www.nmarchive.com
Published in association with The National Archives

Published by

The Naval & Military Press Ltd

Unit 10 Ridgewood Industrial Park,

Uckfield, East Sussex,

TN22 5QE England

Tel: +44 (0) 1825 749494

www.naval-military-press.com

www.nmarchive.com

This diary has been reprinted in facsimile from the original. Any imperfections are inevitably reproduced and the quality may fall short of modern type and cartographic standards.

© **Crown Copyright**

Images reproduced by permission of The National Archives, London, England, 2015.

Contents

Document type	Place/Title	Date From	Date To
Heading	WO95/2891/3 Deputy Assistant Director Ordnance Services		
Heading	52nd Division Dep. Asst Dir. Ord. Services Apr 1918-Apr 1919		
War Diary	Surafend	01/04/1918	30/04/1918
War Diary	Aire	01/05/1918	31/05/1918
War Diary	La Targette	01/06/1918	31/07/1918
War Diary	Houdain	01/08/1918	01/08/1918
War Diary	Maroeuil	02/08/1918	15/08/1918
War Diary	Mingoval	16/08/1918	31/08/1918
War Diary	Boyelles	01/09/1918	16/09/1918
War Diary	Ecoust	17/09/1918	07/10/1918
War Diary	Tincquette	08/10/1918	20/10/1918
War Diary	Thelus	21/10/1918	22/10/1918
War Diary	Henien Lietard	23/10/1918	31/10/1918
War Diary	Beuvry Les Orchies	01/11/1918	08/11/1918
War Diary	Nivelle	09/11/1918	11/11/1918
War Diary	Badour	12/11/1918	15/12/1918
War Diary	Nimy	16/12/1918	23/03/1919
War Diary	Soignies	24/03/1919	30/04/1919

WO95/2891/3
Deputy Assistant Director
Ordnance Services

52ND DIVISION

DEP. ASST DIR. ORD. SERVICES
APR 1918 – APR 1919

WAR DIARY
or
INTELLIGENCE SUMMARY.

Army Form C. 2118.

April 1st - 30th 1918

Vol 1

Place	Date	Hour	Summary of Events and Information	Remarks and references to Appendices
Swafers	1st		Opened Dump at this place to receive all vehicles & artillery of the Div	
	6th		by the 6th Divn was completed & everything handed over to Corp Sup.	
	8th		Embarked on	
	17th		Landed Marseilles, left there the same evening & arrived Rue 16	
			morning of the 20th	
	20th			
	22		Went to Abbeville. Drew 7700 S.B.R's containers, the redemption Lens & Black	
			Saw A.D.O.S. 413 #F Coy R.E. who came on leave. Cavalry submitted weekly	
			A.D.O.S. on Reserve Army, consequently S. was a bit out of Touch with	
			this Units wants	
	23rd		Went to A. every day for sundry indents & sundry Units S.D's when necessary	
	24th		Harness & Saddlery & also any stores possible, Also Saw S.D's arriving	
	25th		& drew for 101 Chief Laundry 10000 drawers, these were drawn & issued	
	26th		also obtained 5 Trucks of Clothing S.D. for Havre but as these were	
			a little late in arriving, all Units were unable to draw equipment	

Army Form C. 2118.

WAR DIARY
or
INTELLIGENCE SUMMARY.
(Erase heading not required.)

Place	Date	Hour	Summary of Events and Information	Remarks and references to Appendices
	29/30		A big proportion of the clothing & the returned to Abbeville. Not sufficient time was allowed at Rue to get all stores for the Div. also a certain quantity of stores useful to been passed to Div. stores & this led to confusion. Left Rue & came to Air.	

Ipswich Capt
DADVS 52 Div
10.5.18

Army Form C. 2118.

WAR DIARY
or
INTELLIGENCE SUMMARY.
(Erase heading not required.)

Instructions regarding War Diaries and Intelligence Summaries are contained in F. S. Regs., Part II. and the Staff Manual respectively. Title pages will be prepared in manuscript.

DADOS 52nd Division

Place	Date	Hour	Summary of Events and Information	Remarks and references to Appendices
Pink	May 1		Opened dump in Riding school at Oise. Set party to Calais for clothing & horse shoes which were urgently required	
	2			
	3		Received stores from Calais & despatched horses to Div Arty	
	4		Sent party to Calais for stores urgently required by Div Arty	
	5		Sent Reproduction to Chatto d'Acq. Cleared dump & Rue & sent stores not required to Beau	
	6		Proceeded to Acq	
	7		Opened dump at Surbaton Camp near Villers an Bois	
	8			
	9		Stores arriving daily from Boral satisfactory	
	10		Remanded in bulk Periscopes for Infantry	
	19			
	20		Talk and other stores arriving	
	21		Demanded 5 Chaffcutters for use of small units	
	22		Stores arriving daily from Boral principally Horse Mule Shoes, Oil Stoves, Bathing	
	26		also quantity of paint for painting vehicles	
	24		Proceeded to Blackpool Siding and selected site for new dump. Dump at Surbaton	
	27		dump superior - no casualties	
	28		Visited Pine and dumps at Blackpool Siding	
	29		Reeves and wires) Electric Signalling Torches to Suffer Bn.	
			Demanded article required for the manufacture of signalling shutters are sparsely	
	30		Nothing of importance	
	31		Boots Clothing to arrived from base - Demanded Pouches for Rifle Grenade	
			Dischargers, Lne 44.41.	

S.R. Winch
D. A. D. O. S. 52 Div. Capt

Army Form C. 2118.

WAR DIARY
or
INTELLIGENCE SUMMARY.
(Erase heading not required.)

D.A.D.O.S
53rd Division
June 1918
Vol 3

Instructions regarding War Diaries and Intelligence Summaries are contained in F. S. Regs., Part II. and the Staff Manual respectively. Title pages will be prepared in manuscript.

Place	Date	Hour	Summary of Events and Information	Remarks and references to Appendices
Ms Varful	1	—	Nothing to report.	
	2	—	1 Truck general stores arrived from Base	
	3	—	Nothing to report.	
	4/5	—		
	6	—	1 Truck Boots, Clothing & Necessaries arrived from Base	
	7	—	1 Truck Boots, Clothing &c (arrived yesterday) issued to Units	
	8	—	1 Truck general stores arrived	
	9	—	Pony wagon to Yola.	
	10	—	2 trucks fuel. Stone bringing from Base. Issue of stones, kerosene	
	11	—	1 Truck SAA. Iron plates rapidly arriving from Base	
	12	—	1 Truck fuel. Stores from Base. Stores went to Units	
	13	—	1 Truck & tools &c from Base. 4 trucks fuel. Money Carts & wheels are manufactured	
	14	—	2 Trucks fuel. Stove. Mortars arrived from Base. Wagon gauge to Units	
	15	—	Issue of Stores sent to Units. Rivet. Gunners Clip opened	
	16	—	2 Trucks fuel. Stores & Trench Mortar Beds from Base	
	17	—	Stores issued to Units	
	18	—	1 Truck Wagon Spares &c from Base	
	19	—	2 Trucks fuel. Spares, types & Cloth Base. Stores went to Units	
	20	—	1 Truck tent propellors from Base. Stores issued to Units	
	21	—	Stores went to Units from Base.	
	22	—	General army to Units	
	23	—	Nothing much to report.	
	24	—	1 Truck field stores from Base	
	25	—	Issue of stores made to Units	
	26	—	Truck of tent propellors from Base	
	27	—	Issue of stores to Units	
	28	—	Nothing to report.	
	29	—		
	30	—		

Army Form C. 2118.

WAR DIARY
or
INTELLIGENCE SUMMARY.
(Erase heading not required.)

DADS 522
July 718
WO 4

Instructions regarding War Diaries and Intelligence Summaries are contained in F.S. Regs., Part II. and the Staff Manual respectively. Title pages will be prepared in manuscript.

Place	Date	Hour	Summary of Events and Information	Remarks and references to Appendices
La Bassée	July 1		2 Trucks Boots C.B. etc and Genl Stores arrived from Base	
	2		Stores (arrived at Unit) issued to Units	
	3		Nothing to report	
	4		1 Truck Camp Kettles, Picketing gear etc arrived from Base	
	5		Issue of Stores proceeding	
	6		Nothing to report	
	7		Nothing to report	
	8		1 Truck Picketing gear, Camp Kettles Equipment & Gen Stores fr Base	
	9		Stores issued to Units	
	10		Nothing to report	
	11		1 Truck Boots, C.B. etc arrived from Base	
	12		1 Truck Socks, Necessaries etc arrived from Base. Stores issued to Units	
	13		3 Trucks Bicycles, Handcarts, Drills and Genl Clothes from Base rec. of Stores to Units proceeding	
	14		Stores issued to Units	
	15		1 Truck Picketing gear, Camp Kettles from Base, Stores issued to Units	
	16		Issue of Stores to Units	
	17		6 Trucks Tents, Stores, Wagons GS, Handcarts arrived from Base	
	18		Stores issued to Units, Standing orders none received	

Army Form C. 2118.

WAR DIARY
or
INTELLIGENCE SUMMARY.
(Erase heading not required.)

July 1918

Place	Date	Hour	Summary of Events and Information	Remarks and references to Appendices
Vargella	July 19		Stores issued to Units. Bars wired to suspend issues	
	20		Nothing to report.	
	21		Bicycles received from Base and issued to Units. Proceeded to Abbeville to select Office Dump. Bars wired accept or such	
	22		Advance party sent to Abbeville	
	23		Remainder of personnel proceeded to Abbeville & area opened Dump.	
	24		Springs turning out tyres from Gun Parks. Arms issued to R.A. Stores received from Gun Parks.	
	25		2 Trucks Spring Stops arrived from Bars & issued to Units. Rose tyres from Gun Parks.	
	26		Stones issued to Units. 16# Gun Lewis issued to Artillery	
	27		Truck Lub. Oils arrived from Gun Parks & issued to M.G.Bn.	
	28		1 Truck Gen'l Stores arrived from Base. Same to Units.	
	29		1 Truck Gen'l Stores arrived from Base. Same to Units proceeding	
	30		Bars wired to suspend issues	
	31		Arranged for Office and Dump in new area.	

S.D. Wind
Major.
D.A.D.O.S. 5th Div. Armoured

WAR DIARY
or
INTELLIGENCE SUMMARY.
(Erase heading not required.)

Army Form C. 2118.

DADOS August 1918 Vol 5

Instructions regarding War Diaries and Intelligence Summaries are contained in F.S. Regs., Part II. and the Staff Manual respectively. Title pages will be prepared in manuscript.

Place	Date	Hour	Summary of Events and Information	Remarks and references to Appendices
Ibadan	1	—	Advance party sent to Maroua.	
Maroua	2	—	Remainder of personnel to Maroua, opened new office and dump.	
	3	—	1 Truck, Clo, etc received. Stores issued to Units. Area shelled no casualties.	
	4	—	Issue of stores to Units proceeding.	
	5	—	2 Trucks, Bicycles, Gas, Resp, Boots and 1 travelling Kitchen from Base.	
	6	—	Stores issued to Units. Area shelled no casualties.	
	7	—	Issue of stores to Units proceeding. Area shelled no casualties.	
	8	—	Area shelled no casualties.	
	9	—	2 Trucks, Clo, Gas, Gen Stores, Bicycles etc arrives from Base. Stores issued to Units.	
	10	—	Issue of stores proceeding.	
	11	—	1 Truck Gen Stores from Base. Stores issued to Units.	
	12	—	Stores issued to Units. 300 pro Gun tops received 9 mules & Ox L.	
	13	—	Issue of stores proceeding. Warning rec'd re stores reserved Base. Orders to suspend issue.	
	14	—	2 Trucks Clo, Boots and Wheels arrives from Base. Stores reserved to Units.	
	15	—	Issue of stores proceeding. Orders dump to pro rail to Kinjana. Base stores to restock rail. Base orders to restock rail.	

(A7031) Wt. W12839/M1293. 75,000. 1/17. D.D. & L., Ltd. Forms/C.2118/14.

Army Form C. 2118.

WAR DIARY
or
INTELLIGENCE SUMMARY.
(Erase heading not required.)

August 1918

Place	Date August	Hour	Summary of Events and Information	Remarks and references to Appendices
Nu ourul	16		Prisoners of personnel to Ningoul, Others rec'd Offrs and dumps.	
	17		Nothing to report	
	18		Nothing to report	
	19		Stores from Paris, various to rec'd from Gun Park.	
	20		1 truck some stores rec'd from Bass Stores issued to Units	
	21		None rec'd. received. Bros issued to Vickers were stores issued to units	
	22		August Party sent to Cony. Trucks and lorries arrived from Bois. dored at Aubigny.	
	23		Personnel of Gun*dumps*, personnel, removed proceeds to Bocourt. Bros issued to Vickers issued.	
	24		Nothing to report	
	25		Transferred & Vickers Gun Boyonet condemned women. Air Civil Artz	
	26		Supplies from 29th Division. Stores rec'd from Gun Park to Units made Vickers issued to Units in demand to Gun. Park and Returned to 91st Bde.	
	27		Stores to Vickers to Units to 18 Pdr. Ammunition to 836 also Stores & Ammo from Gun Park.	
	28		Stores issued to Units. Springs, suggers &c issued from Gun Park Trucks Gun & Stores from Bros	
	29		Stores received to Units.	
	30		Stores, Machine Gun Springs &c. rec'd from Gun Park and various Units	
	31		Stores issued to Units. Machine Gun &c were Received	
			2 trucks 6th Gnd Stores arrived from Paris	

D.A.D.O.S. 52nd Division

Army Form C. 2118.

WAR DIARY
or
INTELLIGENCE SUMMARY.
(Erase heading not required.)

Instructions regarding War Diaries and Intelligence Summaries are contained in F.S. Regs., Part II. and the Staff Manual respectively. Title pages will be prepared in manuscript.

Antros September 1918

Place	Date	Hour	Summary of Events and Information	Remarks and references to Appendices
Boyelles	1	—	Stores through night. Equip & Bottles etc issued to Units. Stores received from Park.	
	2	—	Stores issued to Units.	
	3	—	Machinery S.B. Celebration & 80 O.R. Arr & moved to ship their Equipment to Units.	
	4	—	Stores issued to Units.	
	5	—	2 ton Genl. Stores received from Base. Stores issued to Units.	
	6	—	Stores issued to Units.	
	7	—	Issue of stores proceeding.	
	8	—	Genl. Stores received from Base. Stores issued to Units.	
	9	—	Issue of stores to Units.	
	10	—	1 Truck Clo. etc recd. from Base.	
	11	—	1 Truck Clo. Boots recd. from Base.	
	12	—	1 Truck Rail. Stores recd. from Bgd. Stores passed to Units.	
	13	—	Stores issued to Units. Reps drawn from Gun Park.	
	14	—	1 Truck Genl. Stores and Articles from Base. Issue proceeding.	
	15	—	Stores issued to Units.	
	16	—	1 Truck Clo. and Necessaries received from Base. Warning Order move received. Advance Party sent to Ecoust.	
Ecoust	17	—	Remainder of personnel to Ecoust. Opened new Offices and dumps at Ecoust.	

WAR DIARY or **INTELLIGENCE SUMMARY**
(Erase heading not required.)

Army Form C. 2118.

September 1918

Place	Date	Hour	Summary of Events and Information	Remarks and references to Appendices
Escaut	18		Stores issued to Units	
	19		Issue of Stores proceeding.	
	20		1 Truck Genl. Stores arrived from Base.	
	21		Stores issued to Units	
	22		Issue of stores progressing	
	23		1 Truck. Horse Shoes, Soap etc Bicycle from Base	
	24		Stores issued to Units	
	25		Stores issued to Units	
	26		Nothing to report	
	27		1 Truck Clo. and Genl Stores from Base. Stores issued to Units	
	28		5 Trucks Blankets from Base Manner order from G in Chief	
	29		3 Trucks new to fashion Cl. etc from Base Stores issued to Units	
	30		Stores issued to Units. Darning order. None received.	

30.9.1918

Ipswich Major
D.A.D.O.S. 32nd Division

WAR DIARY or INTELLIGENCE SUMMARY

Army Form C. 2118.

VISION October 1918

Place	Date October	Hour	Summary of Events and Information	Remarks and references to Appendices
	1	-	Advance party to new dump.	
	2	-	Opened new office and workshop. Receiving stores from Gun Park.	
	3	-	Issue of stores proceeding. Stores obtained from Gun Park.	
	4	-	Stores issued to Units.	
	5	-	Stores issued to Units.	
	6	-	Nothing to report.	
	7	-	Closed offices & dump. Proceeded to Blairville.	
Tincques to	8	-	Opened new office and dump at Tincques.	
	9	-	Machine Guns. Demands from Gun Park.	
	10	-	Demands urgent requirement Oil Lub. Clock from Base by agn.	
	11	-	Issues of stoney ways to Units 13th & 1st Heavy German Machine	
	12	-	Gun train from Pit Division. Light Stores arrive to Units	
	13	-	Supplies of Boots & Clo received from Base. Stores arrived from Base	
	14	-	Issue of stores tomorrow. 2 Trucks Genl. Stores arrived from Base	
	15	-	Stores issued to Units.	
	16	-	Boots, General stores received from Base, issued to Units	
	17	-	Machine Guns received from Gun Park & issued to Units	
			1 Truck Clothing received. Issues to Units proceeding.	

Army Form C. 2118.

WAR DIARY
or
INTELLIGENCE SUMMARY.
(Erase heading not required.)

October 1918.

Place	Date	Hour	Summary of Events and Information	Remarks and references to Appendices
Tingry	18	1	Further news of Clothing received 17B could not be made owing to truck moving. 4 Trucks Winter clothing to arrive - reconsigned to near Audruicq	
	19	1	moved to Helis	
Helis	20	1	Nothing to report. Truck General Stores arrived. Nothing to report.	
	21	1	1 Truck General Stores arrived	
	22	1	Trucks received from Turgres arrived. moved to Henin Lietard	
Henin Lietard	23	1	Opened Office and dumps. Sent closer to front.	
	24	1	Clothing Depots etc. issued to units. Moved to Warrenden	
	25	1	Opened Office and dumps at Warrenden	
	26	1	Mr D.A.D.O.S. proceeded to Douai and arranged for temporary storage of stores	
	27	1	Nothing to report	
	28	1	Moved to Ceuvry les Orchies - Opened Office & dump	
	29	1	Stores collected from Douai Dump and sent to units	
	30	1	Bicycles, Soap, thiols etc. Z.D. Boots issued to units	
	31	1	Stores collected from Douai Dump & issued to units	

31/10/18

S.D.Wish
D.A.D.O.S. 52nd Div.

WAR DIARY
or
INTELLIGENCE SUMMARY.
(Erase heading not required.)

Army Form C. 2118.

D.A.D.O.S. 52D
November 1918

Place	Date	Hour	Summary of Events and Information	Remarks and references to Appendices
Bouzincourt Ovillers	1	—	Stores, Clo. etc collected from Divnl. dumps and issued to units	
	2	—	2 Trucks Genl. Stores arrived from Base, issued to Units. Iron screening	
	3	—	1 Lorry filled Boots, Coats etc for Arty. from Divn. Trunk Genl. Stores.	
	4	—	Issued Stoves and Divnl. Clo. to various Units	
	5	—	2 Trucks Oil, Grease, Picketing Pegs etc from Base Stores issued to Units.	
	6	—	2 Trucks Clo. etc from Base Stores issued to Units	
	7	—	Stores issued to Units	
	8	—	Truck picks rehauls, Underclothing from Base, warming orders at Divnl. Railway	
Nivelle	9	—	Advance party to Nivelle opened office + forward dump	
	10	—	Closed Office and dump at Nivelle, moved forward to Fars Canal, unable to cross, parked at Bruille	
	11	—	Crossed canal, moved forward to Mont de Peruwelz	
Badour	12	—	Moved forward to Badour, opened forward Office and dump	

Army Form C. 2118.

WAR DIARY
or
INTELLIGENCE SUMMARY.
(Erase heading not required.)

November 1918.

Place	Date	Hour	Summary of Events and Information	Remarks and references to Appendices
Bavous	13	-	Wired rear dump to send all stores less of Oil, Clo etc and to Units. Truck of horse shoes from Base	
	14	-	Stores arrived from rear dump. Issue of stores to Units.	
	15	-	Demanded Gun Blanket for men & Division stores issued to Units.	
	16	-	Issued horse shoes Clo. & genl stores to Units.	
	17	-	Issue of stores proceeding.	
	18	-	Horse shoes arrived from Base	
	19	-	Stores issued to Units	
	20	-	Blankets Horse rugs arrived from Base. Issue of stores to Units proceeding	
	21	-	2 trucks Genl Stores from Base	
	22	-	Stores issued to Units	
	23	-	Issue of stores proceeding	
	24	-	1 Truck Clo etc arrived from Base. Stores issued to Units	

Army Form C. 2118.

WAR DIARY
or
INTELLIGENCE SUMMARY.
(Erase heading not required.)

November 1918.

Place	Date	Hour	Summary of Events and Information	Remarks and references to Appendices
Baours	25	-	Stores issued to Units	
	26	-	Slow horse shoes. Blankets arriving from Base.	
	27	-	Issue of stores to Units	
	28	-	Stores issued to Units	
	29	-	Trucks, Gent Elves, Chaffcutters, Bags Horse etc from Base. Stores issued to Units	
	30	-	Issues of Stores to Units proceeding.	

S. Prowrich
Capt.
D.A.D.O.S. 52nd Division

30/11/918

Army Form C. 2118.

WAR DIARY
or
INTELLIGENCE SUMMARY.
(Erase heading not required.)

FADS
December 1918

9817

Place	Date	Hour	Summary of Events and Information	Remarks and references to Appendices
Seaford	1	-	Stores issued to Units	
	2	-	Truck general stores arrived from Base	
	3	-	Stores issued to Units	
	4	-	Nothing to report	
	5	-	2 Trucks Boots, Shoes, Clothing etc arrived from Base	
	6	-	Stores issued to Units	
	7	-	Clothing arrived from Base	
	8	-	Stores issued to Units	
	9	-	Stores Trucks Shoes arrived from Base	
			Stores Clothing etc arrived from Base Stores issued to Units	
	10	-	Soap Dubbing etc arrived from Base	
	11	-	Stores & kits to Units proceeding	
			Stores issued to Units	
	12	-	Clothing arrived from Base	
	13	-	Stores issued to Units	
	14	-		

Army Form C. 2118.

WAR DIARY
or
INTELLIGENCE SUMMARY.
(Erase heading not required.)

December 1918

Instructions regarding War Diaries and Intelligence Summaries are contained in F. S. Regs., Part II. and the Staff Manual respectively. Title pages will be prepared in manuscript.

Place	Date	Hour	Summary of Events and Information	Remarks and references to Appendices
Belgium	15		Advance party to Menin	
Menin	16		Opened new office Avenue at Henry Blanket Tents	
			Sent Lorks etc across from Bray	
	17		Stores leaves to Units	
	18		Issue of Stores to Units proceeding	
	19		Nothing Onpost	
	20		Stores general arrives from Bray	
	21		Stores issues to Units	
	22		Issue of Stores proceeding	
	23		Issue of Stores down to Units	
	24		Clothing arrives from Bray	
	25		Some stores arrive from Bray Stores issues to Units	
	26		Stores issues to Units	
	27		Issue of Stores proceeding	

Army Form C. 2118.

WAR DIARY
or
INTELLIGENCE SUMMARY.

(Erase heading not required.)

December 1918

Place	Date	Hour	Summary of Events and Information	Remarks and references to Appendices
Simcy	28	—	Stores issued to Units	
	29	—	Issue of Stores proceeding	
	30	—	Gert Stores, Lewis Stores etc arrived from Base Stores. Issues to Units.	
	31	—	Working preparet.	

Jno Scott
Captain for
D.A.D.O.S. 32nd Division

1/1/19.

WAR DIARY
or
INTELLIGENCE SUMMARY.

Army Form C. 2118.

DADOS 52
January 1918
Vol 10

Place	Date	Hour	Summary of Events and Information	Remarks and references to Appendices
January	1		Nothing to report	
	2		Small Cuno Stores arrived from Base	
	3		Stores issued to French	
	4		Clothing Stores goes etc from Base. Some issued to troops	
	5		Issue of stores this [illegible]	
	6		Issue of Stores proceeding	
	7		" " "	
	8		Coy Stores arrived from Base	
	9		Clothes issued to troops	
	10		Stores issued to troops	
	11		Stores Clo. etc arrived from Base	
	12		Issue of Clo. to troops [illegible]	
	13		Issue of Stores to troops	
	14		Some Stores from Base	
	15		Issue of Stores to troops	
	16		Nothing to report	
	17		Nothing to report. Wagons Carts etc arrived from Base	

Army Form C. 2118.

WAR DIARY
or
INTELLIGENCE SUMMARY.

(Erase heading not required.)

January 1919
Enquires

Instructions regarding War Diaries and Intelligence Summaries are contained in F. S. Regs., Part II. and the Staff Manual respectively. Title pages will be prepared in manuscript.

Place	Date	Hour	Summary of Events and Information	Remarks and references to Appendices
Army	18	-	Stores issued to Units	
	19	-	Stores issued to Units	
	20	-	Vehicles from Base for Artillery	
	21	-	Stores issued to Units	
	22	-	Rect Stores from Base	
	23	-	Reels etc from Base	
	24	-	Stores issued to Units	
	25	-	Issue of Stores proceeding	
	26	-	Horse Shoes from Base	Rec'd Stores mainly B Units
	27	-	Arty Stores & Reels etc from Base	
	28	-	Issue of Stores to Units	
	29	-	Stores issued to Units	
	30	-	Oil & Grease, Oxy etc from Base	
	31	-	Stores issued to Units	

Soldich
S.D.O.O.S. 52nd Division

Army Form C. 2118.

Davos 52D
February 1919
982 11

WAR DIARY
or
INTELLIGENCE SUMMARY.
(Erase heading not required.)

Instructions regarding War Diaries and Intelligence Summaries are contained in F. S. Regs., Part II. and the Staff Manual respectively. Title pages will be prepared in manuscript.

Place	Date	Hour	Summary of Events and Information	Remarks and references to Appendices
Davos	1	—	Stores wired to Guides	
	2	—	Lists of Stores preparing	
	3	—	Clothing Book to be turned from Base	
	4	—	Lists issued to Guides	
	5	—	Supplies arrived from Base	
	6	—	Bicycle arrived from Base	
	7	—	Clothing parts issued to Guides	
	8	—	Stores turned of Guides	
	9	—	Lists of Stores preceding Base — Rec. Stores turned to Units	
	10	—	Corp. Stubbing, more Clues from Base	
	11	—	R.J. Smith 26 out Private for R.J.O. from Base	
	12	—	Lists issued to Guides	
	13	—	Lists of Stores preceding	
	14	—	Group Report	
			Article arrived from Base	
	15	—	Stores issued to Units	

(A 10266) Wt W5300/P713 750,000 2/18 Sch. 52 Forms/C2118/16
D. D. & L., London, E.C.

Army Form C. 2118.

WAR DIARY
or
INTELLIGENCE SUMMARY.
(Erase heading not required.)

February 1919

Place	Date	Hour	Summary of Events and Information	Remarks and references to Appendices
[illegible]	16	—	Boots, Shirts Underclothing etc., 300 prs arrived from Base	
	17	—	More Stores Shirts, Underclothing etc from Base. Stores issued to Units	
	18	—	Stores issued to Units	
	19	—	More Stores arrived from Base. Issue of Kits to Units	
	20	—	Stores issued to Units	
	21	—	Weekly return Stores etc from Base	
	22	—	Clothing received from Base. Kits issued to Units	
	23	—	Boots received from Base. Stores issued to Units	
	24	—	Stores issued to Units	
	25	—	Oil, Grease, & Pickling Grease received from Base	
	26	—	Stores issued to Units	
	27	—	Boots, Clothing etc received from Base. Stores issued to Units	
	28	—	Stores issued to Units	

1-3-1919.

S. Aldwick Capt
D.A.D.O.S. 52nd Division

Army Form C. 2118.

WAR DIARY
or
INTELLIGENCE SUMMARY.
(Erase heading not required.)

March 1919

Instructions regarding War Diaries and Intelligence Summaries are contained in F. S. Regs., Part II. and the Staff Manual respectively. Title pages will be prepared in manuscript.

Place	Date	Hour	Summary of Events and Information	Remarks and references to Appendices
Army	1		Stores issued to Units	
	2		Issue of Stores progressing	
	3		Issued stores etc from Base	
	4		Stores issued to Units	
	5		Stores issued to Units	
	6		Nothing to report	
	7		Nothing to report	
	8		Transit Stores recd from Base	
	9		Stores issued to Units	
	10		Remytn Inspection 10th 197th Bgn 147 AFA Bde	
	11		Nothing to report	
	12		Remytn Inspection of 9th Bde R.A.	
	13		Nothing to report	
	14		Nothing to report	
	15		Recd stores from Base	
	16		Stores issued to Units	

Army Form C. 2118.

WAR DIARY
or
INTELLIGENCE SUMMARY.
(Erase heading not required.)

March 1919

Place	Date	Hour	Summary of Events and Information	Remarks and references to Appendices
Cumil	17	-	Stores issued to Units	
	18	-	Nothing to report	
	19	-	Advance party to Cognac	
	20	-		
	21	-	Nothing to report	
	22	-	Nothing to report	
	23	-	Down the Inspector of Equip. H.Q. O.C. B.Sn except "C" & "D" Sly	
	24	-	Sam onwards (?) Resumed to Cognac, Deputy Inspector 55th Bde B.Sn	
Cognac	25	-	Deputy Inspector 153 & 156 Syn B.Sns	
	26	-	Deputy Inspector from Base left by Q.E., to advance ??? Supplies	
	27	-	Horse shoes Oil & Grease Ropes etc. from Base	
	28	-	Stores issued to Units	
	29	-	Deputy Inspector Ord. Reg. Corp, Sup, Sec HQrs	
	30	-	Stores issued to Units	
	31	-	Stores issued to Units	

Army Form C. 2118.

PARTS 627

April 1919

90 13

WAR DIARY
or
INTELLIGENCE SUMMARY.
(Erase heading not required.)

Instructions regarding War Diaries and Intelligence Summaries are contained in F. S. Regs., Part II. and the Staff Manual respectively. Title pages will be prepared in manuscript.

Place	Date	Hour	Summary of Events and Information	Remarks and references to Appendices
Cognac	1	-	Nothing to report	
	2	-	Chr. Boots etc from Base	
	3	-	Stores issued to Units	
	4	-	Lewis & Vickers processing	
	5	-	Working Parties	
	6	-	Vehicles arrived from Workshops	
	7	-	Issued many Blankets	
	8	-	Boots & Gren Boots from Base	
	9	-	Stores issued to Units	
	10	-	Stores issued to Units	
	11	-	Stores issued to Units	
	12	-	Nothing to report	
	13	-	Nothing to report	
	14	-	Stores received from Base	
	15	-	Issues made to Units	
	16	-	Issues made to Units	

Army Form C. 2118.

WAR DIARY
or
INTELLIGENCE SUMMARY.
(Erase heading not required.)

April 1919

Place	Date	Hour	Summary of Events and Information	Remarks and references to Appendices
Suippes	17		Leave proceeding	
	18		Nothing to report	
	19		Nothing to report	
	20		Stores received from Base	
	21		Leaves made to Units	
	22		Leaves made to Units	
	23		Leaves made to Units	
	24		} Nothing to report	
	25			
	26			
	27			
	28		} Stores received from Base & Issues made to Units	
	29			
	30			

1/5/1919

F Major
OA Dos 52 Div

www.ingramcontent.com/pod-product-compliance
Lightning Source LLC
Chambersburg PA
CBHW081503160426
43193CB00014B/2581